D1442308

MEDIEVAL LIVES

Nun

ROBERT HULL

A+

Smart Apple Media

Smart Apple Media is published by Black Rabbit Books
P.O. Box 3263, Mankato, Minnesota 56002

Printed in the United States

Published by arrangement with the Watts Publishing Group Ltd, London.

Library of Congress Cataloging-in-Publication Data

Hull, Robert, 1935-
    Nun / Robert Hull.
    p. cm.—(Smart apple media. Medieval lives)
    Summary: "Traces the life of a typical nun in medieval times from birth to death, including childhood,
training, and vows taken by nuns. Includes primary source quotes"—Provided by publisher.
    Includes index.
    ISBN 978-1-59920-171-9
    1. Monastic and religious life of women—History—Middle Ages, 600-1500. I. Title.
BX4210.H85 2008
271'.90040902—dc22
                                                                                        2007050617

Artwork: Gillian Clements
Editor: Sarah Ridley
Editor-in-chief: John Miles
Designer: Simon Borrough
Art director: Jonathan Hair
Picture research: Diana Morris

Picture credits:
AKG Images: 29. Austrian Museum of Applied Arts Vienna/Bridgeman Art Library: 25. Bargello Museum Florence/Alfredo Dagli
Orti/The Art Archive: 23. Bibliotheque Municipale Poitiers/Gianni Dagli Orti/The Art Archive: 27. Bibliotheque Nationale
Paris/AKG Images: 37. Bibliotheque Nationale Paris/Giraudon/Bridgeman Art Library: 39. British Library London: 15, 19.
British Library London/The Art Archive : front cover, 21. British Library London/Bridgeman Art Library: 33. British Museum
London/Bridgeman Art Library: 34. Chateau de Versailles/Giraudon/Bridgeman Art Library: 24. Fitzwilliam Museum
Cambridge/Bridgeman Art Library: 35. Erich Lessing AKG Images : 11. Musée de l'Assistance Publique, Hopitaux de Paris/Archives
Charmet/Bridgeman Art Library: 14. Musée Condé Chantilly/Bridgeman Art Library: 10, 13t. Musée de l'Hospice de Villeneuve-les-
Avignon/Gianni Dagli Orti/The Art Archive: 22. Musée Lambinet/Archives Charmet/Bridgeman Art Library: 20. Musée Muncipale
St Germain-en-Laye/AKG Images: 30. Musée des Tapisseries Angers/Lauros Giraudon/Bridgeman Art Library: 38. Museo Nazionale
de Lazzo di Venezia, Rome/AKG Images: 18. Museo Provincial de Bellas Artes Zaragoza/Bridgeman Art Library: 41. Gerhard
Ruf/AKG Images: 9. Topfoto: 13c. Victoria & Albert Museum London/Bridgeman Art Library: 26. Victoria & Albert Museum
London/Eileen Tweedy/The Art Archive: 7, 31. von Linden/AKG Images: 17

9 8 7 6 5 4 3 2 1

CONTENTS

INTRODUCTION

The medieval period of European history is from approximately 1000 to 1500. It was a time of momentous events. In 1066, England was conquered by the Norman French duke William and his men. France and England fought a series of wars called the Hundred Years' War. Christian crusaders fought with Muslim Arab armies over the control of Jerusalem. In 1348, the Black Death, or plague, killed about one-third of the population in Europe.

Feudal Society

At the beginning of this period, European society was feudal. Kings owned the land, granting it to warrior knights, or barons, in return for service in war. Knights rented tenements to those below them—holders of manorial estates, including religious houses, and they in turn rented land in return for money or services to those below them, down to the peasants. But from the thirteenth century onward, the growth of towns, trade and travel, and money transactions started to dissolve this feudal structure.

Although religious orders were not strictly part of feudal society, there was a similar structure in the church, with the pope as king, cardinals as nobles, bishops as knights, and ordinary priests, monks, and nuns as peasants.

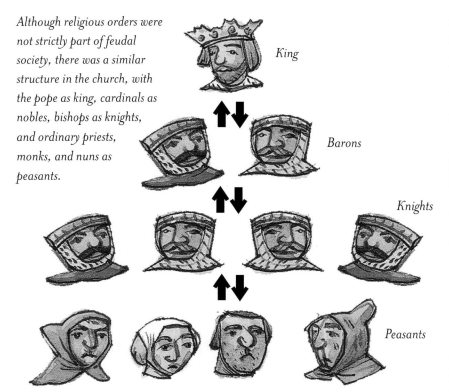

King

Barons

Knights

Peasants

Monastic Life

Almost everyone in medieval Europe believed in a Christian God and followed the teachings of the Roman Catholic Church, which was headed by the pope in Rome. Religion was at the center of their lives. Some people chose to join religious communities, or orders, such as: Benedictine, Carthusian, Cistercian, Cluniac, Dominican, and Franciscan. Each order had monasteries for men and convents—or nunneries—for women.

Religious Communities

Throughout the medieval period, more men than women lived monastic lives. However, a powerful religious revival in the twelfth and thirteenth centuries brought many women into religious communities.

Devoted Women

Some churchmen believed women were particularly suited to the religious life. Johannes Brinckerinck helped found a spiritual movement, Modern Devotion, in the Netherlands. In 1419, he wrote:
❖ *When women apply themselves devoutly they often receive more grace and stand in greater favor with God than men do.* ❖

8

There were only 13 nunneries in England in 1066. During the next 150 years, 120 more were founded.

Many women entered nunneries in devoted dedication; others because marriage was, economically, not an option. Around 1066, most women seemed to marry. However, as the dowry, the wedding gift provided by the father of the bride, became more expensive, parents with several daughters found the price of marriage for each daughter to a man of adequate status beyond their reach. An alternative career, as a nun, required a smaller entry payment. It cost less to marry the Son of God than a mortal man, one wit said.

Vows

Nuns took vows of poverty, chastity, and obedience. Some also promised to remain within the enclosed community. Enclosure meant remaining within the physical confines of the convent. Only a few authorized people were allowed to visit.

Poverty meant no private possessions and, for some orders, no communal possessions except the necessities for survival—a garden to grow food. Chastity meant always remaining a virgin. Obedience involved unquestioning adherence to the instruction of superiors. These ideals were difficult to live up to. It was stressful to live communally, sleep in dormitories, and eat in refectories. This book follows the story of a merchant's daughter who becomes a nun in the fourteenth century.

This medieval Italian fresco depicts Saint Clare (1194–1253), a nun and friend of Saint Francis of Assisi. She founded an order of nuns, the Poor Clares. She is shown in her nun's habit.

BIRTH

The woman is expecting another baby. The father has asked a monk for assistance with a safe birth. The monk has brought two precious relics: pieces of the sail that belonged to Saint Peter's fishing boat on Galilee. The relics will stay with the mother until she safely delivers her child.

After taking communion and saying farewell to her husband, for the time being, the mother-to-be is brought to a large bedroom that is to be the birth chamber. Only the midwife and women of the household are allowed to enter. Candles burn in the room that has been specially draped with rich cloth and carpeted.

Medieval women believed in magical aids for a safe birth. Striking a bell three times at certain moments helped. Semi-precious stones were useful, especially aetites, or eaglestones, which eagles took to their nests to help breeding. Scrolls with promises written on them could be laid across the mother's belly. It also helped to obtain, for a fee, the use of religious relics from the church such as: the Virgin Mary's girdle, a link from Saint Peter's chains, or a finger bone that belonged to Saint Stephen. Relics were believed to ensure a safe delivery of the baby.

Prayer and Preparation

The household prays—the monk prays. For the baby, the prayer is that it will survive long enough to be baptized. For the mother, that she will be safe and survive to be purified in church after 40 days.

This religious picture depicts the birth of John the Baptist. The scene in a wealthy medieval house would have been much the same. The mother recovers in bed from the birth and the baby is about to be washed.

The medieval baby girl would have been baptized in a stone font such as this one from about 1150 in Skjeberg church, Norway.

Baby Nurse

In some areas of Europe, babies from well-off families seem to have been taken to another woman, often a young peasant, to be nursed and fed. Or a wet-nurse would be hired to live in the house. A fifteenth-century Italian priest wrote disapprovingly, saying wet-nursing and fostering is:

❖ *. . . like taking a peach stone from a fine peach tree in San Gimignano and planting it in Siena, where the soil grows thin, poor trees . . . You have brought the stones here, but not the soil. So I say to you women who send your children out to nurse: they will take on the condition of the coarse peasant girls who feed them.* ❖

There is rejoicing and relief in the large house that evening for a baby girl has been born, another daughter, not a male heir. There is a celebration the same night with a minstrel, music, dancing, food, and drink.

The father is a prosperous merchant whose other daughters have not yet taken expensive dowries into marriages. He can easily afford to provide the entertainment and summon a monk who brings relics.

Baptism
The baptism takes place as soon as possible—after two or three days.

According to the church, an unbaptized child is in danger of going to a place where God is not; that is, to hell. The mother is at home, unpurified after the uncleanliness of giving birth, unable to touch anything holy or enter a church for 40 days.

On the church porch, the priest makes signs of the cross on the baby's forehead and asks her in Latin—by speaking to the godparents—whether she renounces Satan and what it is she wants. For the baby to be baptized, the godparents speak on her behalf. They enter the church and go to the font. The priest,

holding the baby, makes more signs of the cross, sprinkles her with holy water from the font, names her, and hands her back to the godparents.

Churching
After 40 days, the mother joyfully participates in a churching service of purification. After her churching, there is entertainment. The servants are invited to share in the excitement and happiness but also hope that the celebrations are not premature; they remember other babies who died.

CHILDHOOD AND EDUCATION

The baby is nursed and cared for by the women of the household. She quickly grows stronger. The mother is soon busy again managing the large household. She sees her new daughter every day, but the baby's daily breast-feeding, washing, dressing, putting-to-bed, and everyday care are the responsibility of the nurse and the women of the household.

Early Years

Women servants play with the baby, rock her in the cradle, sing to her, and give her lots of the kissing and hugging babies need. They watch when she begins to crawl to make sure she is safe.

The baby becomes a toddler, then a young girl. As she grows older, and unlike boys in other families,

she does not go exploring around the town on her own. She goes out with the servants sometimes and with the family to church.

Reading and Writing

By the time she is five, she is learning to read and write at home, like her sisters. Her father found a respectable woman who is knowledgeable and quiet to teach

her; her conversation is pleasing, and she can speak Latin.

Her parents begin to consider the idea that she might continue her learning in the nunnery outside the town. For a modest fee, the nuns accept a few children as pupils. One or two even live in the nunnery. With this in mind, the teacher instructs her in religious matters. Now that she can read, she has books of devotion, including a Psalter, and books about conduct and behavior.

This manuscript illustration shows a medieval school lesson in progress.

The Convent School

Her mother makes the decision, when the girl is seven, to send her to the convent school. She will not board there, not now at least. A servant will take her each day.

She goes to the school. She likes the nuns and the calm atmosphere. There is even a schoolmaster who teaches Latin; his pupils have to speak only Latin in the schoolroom and also in the street! She learns some simple Latin, and she learns to sing. She is taught with other girls and boys from the town, as well as the nunnery's postulants—girls who wish to become nuns. At times, they are joined by professed (committed)

Medieval children learned their letters from a wooden hornbook, which had its written text covered with transparent animal horn to protect it.

nuns who do not understand Latin well enough to sing the services confidently; they even make mistakes reading from their slates.

13

TO THE NUNNERY – POSTULANT

After three or four years at the school, in a room in the outside wall of the convent, the young girl thinks she would like to become a nun. As a first step, she must proclaim her desire to become one and be a postulant, then later a novice. She is only 11; to be a novice, she must be older—13 or so.

Her parents are pleased for her to become a nun. It means one less marriage dowry. She will be cared for and safe in the nunnery. She will have companions in religion, and if she wants to take her final, binding vows when the time comes, she can. If not, she can leave.

Sisters at an island nunnery welcome a novice (left) and receive a sick person into their infirmary (right) in this fifteenth-century manuscript illustration.

If she stays, she will vow to aspire to many things, but three things especially. In humility, she will obey instructions; she will always remain a virgin and praise chastity; she will give up thought of personal possessions. She will be silent most of the time. Talk with visitors or conversation with other nuns is allowed in the locutarium, but silence is expected at most other times. Mealtimes are silent. Nuns listen to readings and use sign language to say, "pass the bread, please."

The Dowry

In the meantime, her father must pay her entry fee. In theory, this is voluntary, but not in practice—although it is smaller than a marriage dowry. He also provides some furniture, including a bed, and a habit—a set of postulant's clothing.

At home, she wore colorful, pretty clothes, made from expensive materials such as silk. Her habit is a white tunic and scapular (a piece of cloth with an opening for the head), a leather belt, a black mantle, and a veil. The design is simple and the wool is coarse, unfinished, and not dyed. She has to wear the full habit when she sleeps too.

The other three young postulants are from nearby. Their fathers are merchants or farmers with large houses, but not mansions.

Others in the Nunnery

It surprises her that not all the nunnery's inhabitants are nuns. There are two or three older women who are not professed, as well as two widows, one with a daughter living with her as a postulant. Three girls between the ages of six and nine board in the nunnery. Their families pay well for their keep and board, so the prioress accepts them, though the bishop will probably demand that they leave when he visits.

There are women from poorer families too, not nuns, who have taken vows. They are lay sisters, the nunnery's working women.

Some girls are unhappy here. After a year, they will be given the opportunity to decide whether they want to take the nun's vows or not. They will leave.

Postulant Gift

A postulant usually gave a gift of money or property to the nunnery, as she would bring a dowry to a marriage, but smaller. A dowry insufficient for marriage might suffice for the nunnery. The Countess of Warwick left 200 marks in gold to Jane Newmarch:

❖ *. . . to bear all costs as for bringing her into Saint Kathryn's, or wherever she will be else.* ❖

A rector of Brompton, Robert de Playce, made this bequest:

❖ *I bequeath to the daughter of John de Playce my brother 100 shillings for an aid towards making her a nun.* ❖

Language Trouble

The sisterbook of the convent at Diepenveen in the Netherlands records this sad story about Liesbeth van Heenvliet, who entered the convent at the age of 10:

❖ *Sister Elsie Hasenbroecks had ordered her not to speak Dutch without permission. It happened that during the night she became ill and had no basin or container to be sick in. She did not dare speak Dutch, but could not speak Latin. So, producing the nearest to a Latin sound she could, she cried out, "Sister, lackus basinus!"* ❖

In this fourteenth-century manuscript, the abbess (chief nun) cuts the hair of a postulant.

15

It will take time for the future nun to get used to not seeing her family and to the convent's stern rule of silence.

She quickly becomes familiar with areas of the convent she did not visit as a pupil: the churchyard and cross-shaped stone church inside the high wall, the bellhouse by the church, the prioress's rooms next to it, and the cloister where, in the center of it all, she can walk and meditate.

Convent Buildings

By the church is the chapterhouse where the nuns discuss the affairs of the convent—one of the few times the nuns are allowed to talk. On another side of the cloister are the refectory, where everyone eats, the adjacent kitchens, and the sleeping quarters or dorter. Close to the dorter are the latrines and the lavatorium, or washing areas, placed over the stream that flows through.

She discovers the hall. Across the space of the great court is the infirmary with its own chapel, the lodging house for visitors, and the locutarium or parlor where nuns can receive certain visitors (usually family members). At certain times, conversation is permitted on religious subjects and in the presence of senior nuns.

Medieval Facts

Some nunneries had small separate quarters for permanent paying guests, like the widows of those who gave generously to the nunnery. These paying guests were called corrodians. They attended church, seeing the elevation of the host at mass, but could not sit in the nuns' choir. Sometimes viewing galleries were built at one end of the church for the corrodians or any other seculars who were present.

In their spare time, the nuns walk and read in the convent's cloister (covered walk).

The convent of Fontenay in France was founded in 1119. Shown here are the convent buildings with the church on the right.

Farm Buildings

Her mother had described those places, but the schoolroom was well away from the outbuildings and sheds. She was not prepared for the noise of the pigs, lambs, and dogs, which she can hear even from inside the church. She had expected calm and quiet, not the ring of metal from a smithy, carpenters' hammers, or horse-drawn carts rumbling in and out through the gatehouse. The smells of cooking, baking, and brewing were like those at home.

She watches lay sisters seeing to the animals, washing, mending, and cleaning shoes. She catches glimpses of the priests going to and from their rooms over the gatehouse and in chambers in the outer courtyard.

She peers into the stables, the kiln, the milkhouse, and the granary. She finds her way to the garden and the orchard and the small courtyard for the nuns only.

She thinks how all this huddles inside walls that no nun ventures beyond without permission. She wonders whether, if she does become a nun, she will ever step outside these walls again. For now at least, she is free to come and go with the lay sisters working in the fields, like the other boarding children.

Chapter of Faults

The chapterhouse was for non-spiritual meetings of the nunnery. The chapter of faults was a regular meeting of the entire convent. Nuns admitted their faults and were asked by the prioress if they wished to accuse others. The prioress decided on punishments. Salome Sticken, a fifteenth-century prioress at the convent at Diepenveen, in the Netherlands, inflicted various humiliations on offenders:

❖ *She castigated those sisters by making them wear humble clothing and torn and patched surplices and veils. She instructed someone to wear an apron on her head or use buttons from old nightshirts as a paternoster [rosary] . . . She would give them tasks like begging for bread at other tables in the refectory, or kissing the feet of sisters, or asking forgiveness or submitting to being beaten.* ❖

TAKING THE VEIL – NOVICE

At 13, after two years of living freely among the nuns, the young postulant decides she would like to enter the community and "take the veil" as a novice. The entire convent gathers in the chapterhouse to see her address the prioress. The prioress asks the young postulant, "What is your request?"

She has been well prepared: "I wish for the mercy of God and to join the community of nuns."

After more questions and answers, the prioress takes her hands in her own, "On behalf of God and ourselves, we receive you here and grant you fellowship with us."

"Amen," says everyone, and they fuss decorously around her.

Two Holy Nuns *by the Master of San Jacopo – an Italian painting of 1399.*

Investiture as a Novice

There is a ceremony of investiture at the altar in the chapel. The new novice receives her habit, not the habit of a professed nun, but a white veil and sleeveless scapular – a long choir tunic. To remind her that her past is rejected, she is asked to walk on the fur-lined cloak she brought with her to the convent.

The novice learns about being a nun. She is placed in the care of a mistress of novices. Her guidance will be partly moral to teach her how novices should behave and comport themselves obediently and humbly toward their seniors. She will also learn how to chant the eight daily services in Latin, how to sing loudly and softly, and any other skills that nuns need, such as embroidery.

Medieval Facts

In the twelfth century, there was probably no uniform habit for nuns. A ruling of Saint Benedict had stressed the importance of plain clothing but did not mention color. A decree of 1235, from the General Chapter of the Church, stipulated a cloak or cowl and a black veil. Dress generally was somber, even dowdy. Nuns used only undyed inexpensive cloth of black, brown, white, or gray. Within the same Cistercian order, some nuns were known as "white nuns" while others were known as "black nuns."

The program of religious training for the novice of fourteenth-century Windesheim Convent in the Netherlands was part social, part moral, part spiritual:

❖ *And Katharina taught Griete how she should humble herself before her sisters . . . and how she should go to them in silence and subjugation and be attentive to them, and how she should burden her heart with daily contemplation of the suffering of our Lord.* ❖

Profession as a Nun

When she is 15, the novice is offered a choice. She can leave the convent or, by composing a letter, profess formally her desire to become a nun. She writes her letter, vowing to be obedient, embrace poverty, and remain a virgin. The novices who cannot write have their letters written for them, which they sign with a cross.

In the ceremony of profession in the chapel, the novice lies prostrate before the altar, her new habit waiting beside her. After it is consecrated with holy water, she removes her old habit and puts on the new one. She is veiled again, this time in black. Standing by the altar, she reads her letter aloud, kisses it, and kneels again on the altar steps. Mass is sung.

God and the saints look down on nuns in this thirteenth-century manuscript painting. The image at the bottom left depicts a nun in charge of two novices. She holds a birch rod to administer discipline.

In her fifteenth-century *Chronicle and Necrology of Corpus Domini*, Sister Riccoboni of Venice tells the story of Lucia Tiepolo, known for her preoccupation with virginity, who took the:

❖ [Benedictine] *habit at the age of 11 and lived in it for more than 80 years . . . From the moment she was enclosed she never wanted to see a man's face. When doctors or teachers came, she fled; sometimes she could not escape quickly enough on account of her age, so she covered her face with a scapular. The young women asked her: "Why do you flee like that?" She replied: "My dear daughters, even now I fear for my virginity."* ❖

DAILY LIFE –
THE OFFICES

The new nun is fervent in prayer, the praise of God, and spiritual exercises. Her days celebrate abstinence from normal pleasures and commitment to her vows of poverty, chastity, and obedience. For her, the fullest expression of devout spirituality is the daily reciting or singing of the eight daily services—or "offices."

The Nuns' Choir

At each office, she enters the church with the others, bows in front of the altar, and takes her place in the nuns' choir. The nuns are "dead to the world" and perform their liturgical tasks—singing, chanting, and praying—out of sight of the world in the nuns' choir. Their choir, in the chancel, is raised like a gallery and physically separated from the canons below them who perform the sacraments and from other worshippers in the nave.

The new nun is aware that beyond the screen, which hides the nun's choir, are the lay sisters. Further back are the permanent residents, the corrodians, with the rest of the lay people, convent guests, villagers, estate workers, and so on. Of course, these lay worshippers are more likely to be present during daylight hours than when the nuns begin or end their long day of worship.

Within her community, the abbess was all-powerful. This is the thirteenth-century crozier of the abbesses of a Cistercian convent in France. Normally, only bishops carried this symbol of authority.

20

Rules for nuns set out how they should behave as enclosed nuns worshipping communally. There is even a Nuns' Rule for avoiding rude behavior after lauds:

❖ *None shall push up against another willfully, nor spit on the stairs as they come up or down — unless they tread it out forthwith.* ❖

The Offices

The first office, matins, is at midnight in summer and an hour later in winter. It is sung with the lauds. The nuns go to bed for two or three hours, till the office of prime at about 5:00 A.M. or at sunrise.

The weekly chapter of faults is held on the appropriate day. First, there are prayers. Then, the prioress details faults in the nuns' religious observances and asks them to confess their own faults and inform the chapter of other nuns' faults. The new nun dares not say anything about others and waits in trepidation for her own conduct to be faulted. But she is newly professed, and no one speaks badly of her.

Throughout the day, the other offices are observed. Terce is at 7:00 A.M., sext at 9:00 A.M., mass at 10:00 A.M., nones at 2:00 P.M., community mass or vespers is in the late afternoon, and compline is at 6:00 P.M. or 7:00 P.M. in winter and an hour later in summer.

Nuns singing in the choir of their church from an early fifteenth-century manuscript.

THE INNER LIFE

The nun intensely feels the meaning of what she sings and says during the religious services. The hours in the choir are the most significant of her day. But she aspires in other ways as well—to total adherence to her vows and the renunciation of worldly pleasure. The pleasures of food and speech, for instance, are suspiciously worldly, and the temptation to enjoy them is best fended off by extreme abstinence.

One method of spiritual self-education that some literate nuns pursued was to collect uplifting quotations from religious books. These *rapiarola* (collections of extracts) or *libelluli* (little books) were sometimes disapproved of because they were individual collections, so not communal. The Dutch nun, Zweder van Rechteren, from the convent at Windesheim:

❖ *. . . loved the scriptures with such passion that she kept on her person little scrolls, some no longer than a finger, some shorter . . . She carried them in her purse and called them her "shields" against evil.* ❖

The coronation of the Blessed Virgin; *painted in 1453 by Enguerrand Quarton. Images such as this assisted nuns with their prayers.*

Exercises

Most sisters devise personal exercises to help them in their devotions. They do these exercises because they wish the mind to be flooded with the divine every moment of the day, giving the devil no opportunity to sneak in.

One sister prostrates herself before Christ as soon as she wakes. Another has a routine of so many exercises—repeating memorized texts and intensely contemplating one moment in Christ's life—that others can tell the time by her movements and speech.

Abstinence

Abstinence frees the soul for God. The nun has renounced the world for the cloister, and marriage with a man to live as the bride of Jesus Christ. She is overjoyed to be near Him when the Eucharist brings her "the Body and Blood of Christ." For some, abstinence is difficult, and they punish themselves. They fast, pray ceaselessly without sleeping, even beat each other with whips.

Clare of Assisi, who founded the Second Franciscan Order (or order of Poor Clares), often fasted severely, taking no food three days every week and little food on the others.

Sister Riccoboni, in the chronicle of the Venetian convent of Corpus Domini, 1395-1436, mentions certain sisters as worthy of special praise for their devotions:

❖ *These women practiced great abstinence. Many dragged their mattresses away and slept upon bare planks . . . They frequented the choir so much they could hardly wait to go to the office. Some of them told me that when they entered the choir, they seemed to see an angel who led them in singing. When one sister was in ecstasy, she saw white puffs like cotton issue from the mouths of the sisters as they sang. She also saw the devil waiting eagerly to see if anyone left out a syllable, to make a note of it.* ❖

One or two sisters practice humility by "stealing" work—often the worst work, such as cleaning the lavatorium or slaughtering animals. The sisters sneak in beforehand so that the work is already done when the duty nuns arrive.

Reading

Apart from the offices, the most important spiritual activity for the young nun is silently reading devotional books and copying extracts. She enjoys the group read-aloud in which one nun reads aloud.

Private meditation, prayer, and reading—for those who are literate —are fitted in between communal attendance at the offices. About an hour-and-a-half is set aside for reading—before vespers and after the evening meal. Nuns who wish to read more, as the young nun does, in their free time on Sundays or on feast days need the prioress's permission.

The young nun knows she must take care that reading does not become a pleasure of a worldly kind.

Some aids to devotion could be three-dimensional. This ivory sculpture of the Virgin and Child dates from the end of the thirteenth century.

DAILY ROUTINE

The nun finishes her breakfast of bread and ale in silence at about 5:30 A.M. She tidies and cleans her cubicle in the dorter (the communal sleeping area). After her private prayers and meditation, she attends the offices. Then it is time for dinner.

Mealtime

The young nun and a few others sometimes eat as a "family" in the cellaress's room. It is a relief to escape the difficult nuns, such as the former prioress who shows her "humility" by grabbing the least tasty bits of food before anyone else starts eating.

The nun's two meals a day are cooked and served by lay sisters. There is meat sometimes and always on feast days—of which there are more than a hundred! Her drink is nunnery-brewed ale and sometimes wine. Nuns are allowed only bread and water on Fridays and other fast days, though novices eat proper food.

This picture of nuns dining is much later than our period (ca.1710), but the scene probably did not change that much. A sister reads aloud (left) as the others eat in silence.

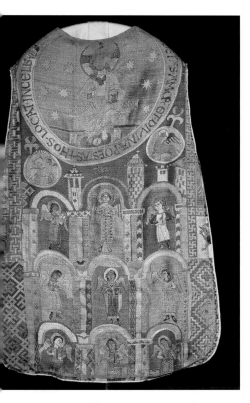

A chasuble (garment for a priest) made by nuns in the thirteenth century.

Work

In the afternoon, every nun is engaged in useful work. The young nun teaches postulants, and girls and boys from nearby, to read and write. There are also children whose fathers have gone on crusade, leaving wives and children in the nunnery. This practice worries the bishop—as all boarding does. Girls and small boys have even slept in the dorter despite letters forbidding this.

Some nuns spin or weave, others embroider vestments—religious garments. One or two nuns are engaged in copying religious texts. There is also work to do in the convent garden and in the orchard. But apart from nuns on official nunnery business, no one goes to work outside the walls. The work needed in the fields—such as haymaking and tending animals—is done by the lay sisters.

Silence and Signs

After compline, there is a short supper. Speaking is not allowed, but sign language is permitted. One nun flaps her hands to indicate, "Please pass the fish." Another nun moves her forefinger up and down her thumb to indicate, "Wine, please."

Nuns on nunnery business out in the world sometimes see something worth retelling. But news such as:
"I saw the cellaress riding behind

the chaplain on his horse this afternoon," is difficult to relate—even using all of the 106 signs in the book.

After dinner it is straight to bed, in the dorter, though some nuns meet to talk. Sleepless nuns must not get out of bed.

ENCLOSURE

The nun has become "dead to the world." She is cut off from the world emotionally. She is not free, for instance, to give or receive the kind of love that she knew with her family. She hardly ever sees any of her family now. A nun's love is exclusively for God.

She is also cut off from the world physically. Her convent is enclosed and separated, as much as it can be, from the outside world. She hears that some nunneries attempt complete enclosure where the sisters try to support themselves entirely from working their own land. They usually struggle and, in extreme cases, begin to starve and need to be helped.

A fifteenth-century tapestry depicts the search for spiritual truth. The two nuns in the middle are enclosed within their convent.

Total Enclosure

Total enclosure means the nunnery does not hold land or property. The nuns strictly stay inside the convent walls and do not go out even to collect alms. This also means that this type of nunnery cannot support itself. It cannot be both contemplative—doing little or no work beyond observing spiritual rule—and totally enclosed or cut off physically from the world around them. If their work does not feed them, and they have no contact with people outside, how can they survive?

Even when nunneries possess land and an income, enclosure can be extreme. The young nun learns of a convent that has only one external door—it is placed high on a wall and can be reached only by a ladder. Food and other goods are brought in using a horizontal wheel, or rota, like a revolving tray.

Attempts were made throughout the medieval period to compel nuns to stay in their convents. In 1298, Pope Boniface VIII made a decree in a document called *Periculoso* for short. All nuns, including prioresses, were to remain perpetually enclosed in their nunneries, unless gravely ill, and receive no visitors except by special license:

❖ *. . . so that being altogether withdrawn from public and mundane sights, and all opportunity for wantonness removed, they may more diligently preserve for Him in all holiness their souls and bodies.* ❖

When the Bishop of Lincoln visited Markyate to put this into effect, the nuns chased him off, throwing the document at his head.

Saint Radegund retreats from the world into her nunnery as depicted in an eleventh-century French manuscript.

Farms and Fields

This nunnery, though, has farms and fields to support it—as well as tolls and tithes, rents, and fines. It was founded with money from a bequest. Since then, it has acquired more farms and land. It functions as a manor. Tenants hold land that nunnery officials manage while the nunnery stays enclosed and focuses on the spiritual life.

Even then, there is the question of how the nunnery should relate to the men it relies on and employs and to those in the outside world with whom it has economic ties. Should a steward or shepherd or carpenter live within the bounds of the convent? Which sisters, if any, should meet the reeve or any other man?

Enclosure was often physically absolute. The Corpus Domini convent in Venice had one door. That door had three locks; each of the three keys was held by a different nun.

CELLARESS AND LIBRARIAN

After several years in the nunnery, the nun takes up the position the prioress wishes her to have—cellaress. In this medium-size convent of about 40 nuns, the cellaress is one of the obedientiaries—officials with particular responsibilities.

The other obedientiaries are: a sub-prioress who assists the prioress; a treasuress who collects rents and fees and pays bills; a chantrist who looks after the music and the running of church services; a sacrist who takes charge of all the church fabric, candles, altar cloths, and so on; an almoness in charge of charity; a chambress in charge of clothes; and a kitcheness in the kitchen.

The Cellaress

The cellaress looks after the food and drink of the convent, storing items from the market and the nunnery's farms—organizing its bakery and brewery. She arranges meals and engages cooks and servers. The nun is proud to serve God in those ways.

The prioress is pleased that her cellaress is a dedicated nun who will not abuse her freedom when she goes outside the nunnery to the marketplace, the farms, or the shops in town. She is levelheaded, not silly or frivolous when she meets the men she must speak to outside the nunnery walls.

A Library

The cellaress is also eager to buy books for the nunnery and take care of them, so she takes on this secondary responsibility. In modest-sized nunneries, roles are often doubled up. Although there is no official librarian, it helps to have someone responsible for books, parchment, and writing utensils.

The nun realizes that aspects of true spirituality are neglected in

Limitations might be imposed on what nuns could read or write. In 1455, the prioress of Windesheim in the Netherlands was banished by the General Chapter, apparently for encouraging "mystical" literature. The resolution displacing her says:

❖ *No nun or sister, no matter what her status, may . . . copy books which contain philosophical teaching or revelations . . . on penalty of imprisonment . . . It is the responsibility of all to ensure that they are burned as soon as they are found.* ❖

Books relating mystical experiences—revelations—had been the most characteristic religious women's literature.

Nunneries had libraries, but seldom much money to buy books. In 1372, William Wokkyng was found guilty of ambushing, with seven accomplices, a certain rector. He robbed the rector of three horses, two girdles harnessed with silver, and books worth £10. One of the books, worth about £3, was later sold to the nunnery at Dartford. Evidently, they were interested in the kind of books that secular clergymen read.

this nunnery. However, the life of the spirit flourishes strongly in others—especially in the reading of spiritual works copied and translated from Latin into the vernacular. Most nuns cannot read Latin, but are willing to try master-works of the spirit such as *The Revelations of St. Bridget* in their own language.

One or two nuns who are deeply engaged in this study also copy manuscripts for others to read. The cellaress is translating an ancient literary work, *Distichia Catonis*, into English verse from the Latin.

A well-educated nun writes at a desk in this fifteenth-century woodcut.

The outside world enters the nunnery in various ways, because the nunnery is part of the world. Local people make bequests to the convent; a croft or pasture is left to the priory in return for the singing of a weekly mass. The nunnery's church is also the parish church; the convent uses one side, the parish the other.

The nunnery needs villagers to work as its officials—steward, bailiff, reeve, and others. It needs peasants to plow, sow, reap, and tend to its animals. The cellaress meets them all.

Visitors from the Outside World

The convent receives visitors. The bishop calls. The cellaress and obedientiaries are involved with buying goods for the nunnery such as fabric, candles, and building materials. Merchants stop to inspect fleeces from the convent's flock.

A nun (middle) watches a conjuror perform a magic trick in this painting by Hieronymus Bosch (ca. 1450–1516).

Sometimes, family members visit for a brief hour and can talk in the locutarium, if a companion is present. The cellaress's sisters flaunt their latest clothes and jewels. Perhaps once a year, the nun's family is allowed to have dinner with her and bring news of the world. She has little news herself, except the sad tale of a woman living in the nunnery who has heard of the death of her husband on crusade.

Nuns in the World

The tide of affairs flows out, taking
obedientiaries into the world, on
nunnery business. The prioress and
sub-prioress ride off to see lawyers
and auditors, usually appointed
from the nuns' families. The
prioress is called to see the bishop
or invited to gatherings in the
town, which she says she attends in
the interests of the nunnery. Useful
bequests and endowments might
follow such contacts.

And of course, the local women
engaged as lay sisters are out and
about daily in the fields and on the
roads. They come and go
frequently.

Nuns are also permitted, perhaps
once a year, to visit their families
and friends, especially when they
are ill. This is a new idea and not

Out in the world—a prioress on her horse, from a manuscript of Geoffrey Chaucer's
The Canterbury Tales.

one that the bishop encourages.
Nuns should never go on travels
among secular people, stay in
common lodging houses, and hear
scurrilous tales and bawdy
songs on the road. But, of course,
when discipline is relaxed these
things happen.

PRIESTS AND NUNS

Nuns have left the world and company of men, but they are closely surrounded by it. Men drive the carts that clatter in and out through the gatehouse all day long. Plowmen, shepherds, haywards, foresters, and ditchers run the farms whose produce and rents enable the nuns to live for God.

The Priest's Spiritual Assistance

Men are needed for the nuns' spiritual work. Nuns cannot hear the confessions of other nuns or receive the Eucharist from them. Only priests are permitted to administer those sacraments. Confession to the priest is made without eye contact with him, through a grille.

The priests are also valuable spiritual advisors. At certain times in the week, one of them speaks to the nuns on specific subjects. The young cellaress finds this advice helpful and makes notes of what is said.

Latin

The priests read Latin documents sent to the prioress. The prioress knows some Latin, but not enough. She knows much less than her cellaress. Priests occasionally perform menial tasks, too, like washing down the altar. The priests live, dine, and sleep in their own quarters, apart from the nuns, but inside the walls of the nunnery in the gatehouse rooms and in chambers in the outer court.

There is also a bishop. The prioress is mistress of the nunnery and has power there, but its control and direction is ultimately in the bishop's hands. He sends the prioress regular letters reminding her that the nuns should not wear jewelry, be seen in the town, own pet dogs, or take a favorite hawk into church.

On the other hand, sometimes the bishop has had to restrain the nuns from excesses of devotion that might damage their health.

Danger

For the nun, men are also a danger and a threat to her vows. She goes among the world of men more than any other nun, but she avoids all unnecessary speech, eye contact, and chance encounters. She knows how easily lapses can occur—and rumors circulate.

Shocking things are indeed seen occasionally. At times, the worst of stories will circulate in shocked whispers of nuns who have run off with minstrels or nuns who have become pregnant by priests.

> ### Naughty Chaplain
>
> Chaplains occasionally displeased the nuns they served. Sir Henry, chaplain of Gracedieu in 1440-1441, goes out haymaking with a cellaress. In the evening, she rides back behind him on his horse. He:
> ❖ . . . busies himself with unseemly tasks, cleaning the stables and going to the altar without washing, so staining his vestments. ❖

Naughty neighbors: in this manuscript picture, a monk and a nun are put in the stocks (a punishment device that pinned the legs) for being too familiar with each other.

POVERTY AND PERSONAL POSSESSIONS

The young woman gave up all her personal property when she became a nun. She gave it to the nunnery to be held in common. Clothing, rings, jewels, pets, food, and allowances of money were forbidden to be in her possession. Gifts from her family are permitted, but these are held by the prioress as communal property.

At the beginning of her time in the nunnery, not even her habit was her own. When the one she was wearing needed washing, she took another, newly cleaned, from the common pile.

A rich thirteenth-century brooch. Nuns could not own such fine items.

Poultry Problems

Allowing personal property in a nunnery created difficulties: even hens could be a problem. Visiting St. Aubin in Normandy, in 1265, a bishop noted that:

❖ *Because several of the nuns keep cocks and hens and often quarrel over them, we ordered that all cocks and hens were to be fed alike and kept in common and the eggs distributed equally among the nuns and that hens should sometimes be given to the sick to eat in the infirmary.* ❖

Two years later, he notes that nothing has been done "about the poultry."

Aspiring to the Ideal

The ideal was always hard to live up to. It is hard to manage with nothing you can call your own. It has now been agreed that there is no point leaving family gifts and bequests—money, rings, chalices, candlesticks, manuscripts—hidden in dark boxes. Individual nuns can now keep them. Now that they have these items, some nuns even want keys for their boxes.

Now there is private property in the nunnery. There is also money for all nuns to spend. It has been agreed that each nun should have a small annual allowance for clothes. Those with only this allowance can supplement it by knitting and embroidering things that they can sell—such as silk purses—to women from the village or to each other.

Money

With their clothing allowances, some nuns—against the rules—buy food from women who come

Female saints are depicted on a page from an early sixteenth-century prayerbook—the sort of lavish item that a nun from a wealthy family might have been allowed to keep.

to the windows or slip into town on the excuse of visiting a sick friend or relative and run up debts at shops. And now that some nuns sometimes eat their own food in "families" or groups separate from those in the refectory, it seems that private money and property may not help communal living.

Although the cellaress is a devout nun, she never totally succeeds in being able to resist her attraction to clothes and jewelry.

The cellaress sees that the idea of property is changing. But even she hardly notices that, like all the nuns, she feeds "her" hens and collects "her" eggs from them. However, she does realize how easily quarrels start over eggs laid in the "wrong" nest.

Inspector of Nunneries

Visiting nunneries in Germany in the fifteenth century, Johann Busch found that nearly all the nuns owned property in various ways. Some had money and rents from land. Nearly all had their own private cooking and dining utensils. Busch describes how, in the course of an inspection, one nun tried to defend her private property. As he went down to the cellars where they kept "their beer and other private allowances," the last nun said to him:

❖ *You go down first, father, for my cellar is the same as those of the other sisters.* ❖

He did so. But when he went down, she suddenly clapped the trapdoor over his head and stood on it.

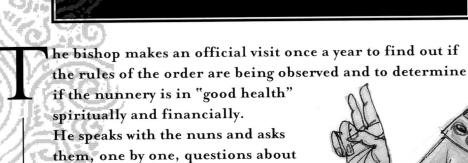

A VISITATION

The bishop makes an official visit once a year to find out if the rules of the order are being observed and to determine if the nunnery is in "good health" spiritually and financially. He speaks with the nuns and asks them, one by one, questions about life in the nunnery.

Lapses

The bishop is told who has gone out without permission or has missed a service. He finds out who talks, who sleeps late, who dawdles near the priest, and who has ridden on horseback with the reeve.

Such offenses are common. This year, there are more worrisome problems. The cellaress has described how nuns can now make small purchases of clothing and other items; now they want keys for their boxes. One or two have been observed wearing rings.

Sick nuns could be better cared for in the infirmary. However, they seem to have no more food than the others, although money has been set aside to buy it. They have even been criticized in their absence at the chapter of faults.

The local bishop visited convents to make sure rules were being followed.

Silence

It seems the fundamental rule of silence is not observed in the church, the cloisters, the refectory, or the dorter. It seems there is surreptitious chatter going on behind every pillar.

The most serious offense is that divine service is performed inadequately. There is giggling and talking during offices; nuns doze off or leave early with an excuse. Snoring has been heard.

And frequently, the bishop finds, the services are hurried through, words are mispronounced, and some nuns have not troubled to discover the meaning of the Latin they sing and speak. There has also been gossiping and drinking after compline.

The Out-of-Favor Prioress

The bishop discovers that the prioress is neglecting her duties. She also has guests to dinner for which she dresses up, curls her hair, and wears furs and jewelry. She even goes out riding.

She lets the sub-prioress meet the nuns in the chapterhouse to take advice about the business of the convent, then makes decisions on her own on important matters that concern everyone, such as which merchants shall handle the convent's crop of fleeces.

The nuns say she has let things slide. Woods have been sold to make money, but the leaky church roof lets rain in. Their worn clothes have holes. They hold up their gloved hands to show him.

Convents were often visited by royalty, as shown in this manuscript illustration.

The bishop listens to all the complaints and writes down that the nunnery is undergoing a crisis. He also knows from the treasuress that no important bequests have been made recently.

DIFFICULT TIMES

The plague of a few years ago took the lives of several nuns. Many workers in the fields died, too. Since then, the cellaress feels nothing has been the same. She wonders what the future holds. The nunnery still owns all its farms, mills, markets, and manor court, but like other manors, it is falling on hard times. In particular, the bequests of land and property from local people have almost ceased.

Famines and plagues were viewed by medieval people as manifestations of God's anger against the sinful.

Food

Not even the nunnery food, which she is responsible for, is as good as it was. At times, harvests have failed and only bread, cheese, and ale have appeared on the table. The nuns have had to provide some food themselves, donated by friends or family. They wonder aloud whether the prioress is still eating well in her rooms and whether the canons' daily fare is as meager as their own.

The bad harvests may be partly to blame, but other aspects of the nunnery's economy are faltering. The fleeces are not fetching the prices they once did. Rent revenue is falling and comes in more slowly. Work drags out. Ditching, fencing, and building repairs are not done promptly.

Poor Management

There were incompetent or uncaring prioresses who brought near ruin on their religious houses and prompted complaints from the nuns during bishops' visitations. At Ankerwyke, in 1441, one nun complained that the prioress:

❖ . . . *furnishes not nor for three years has furnished fitting habits to the nuns, so that they go about in patched clothes.* ❖

Another said that she had no bedclothes:

❖ . . . *insomuch that she lies in the straw.* ❖

In 1253, the nuns of St. Mary, in Chester, wrote to Queen Eleanor begging her to confirm the election of a prioress to their:

❖ . . . *miserable convent, amid its multiplied desolations; for we are so greatly reduced that we are compelled every day to beg abroad our food.* ❖

Clothing

The nunnery's difficulties affect the nuns directly and personally. Clothing is a particular problem. Each nun has had only one pair of shoes a year recently, a tunic every three years or so, and the last change of cloak was six years ago. When their clothes become tattered, they are no longer replaced.

It is often cold and damp in the nunnery. In the winter months, older nuns feel the cold. It is not surprising that some of the younger nuns have started to receive legacies of clothing from their parents.

The cellaress and the more concerned nuns discuss all kinds of explanations. The prioress cannot manage her household properly. The alterations done in the last few years have been too costly and ambitious. Some farmers get away with not paying their rents. Bequests have stopped.

A stern sister in her seventies says that it is God's will that the nuns should be punished for failing to live according to their vows.

War was an ever-present threat to the peace and stability of the community. An army sacks a town in this fifteenth-century painting.

DEATH

The cellaress is still in her forties, but she has become ill by constant worry about how to keep the nunnery supplied with food and drink. Her constitution has been undermined by not only the cold and damp but by too much riding out in the world.

The prioress suggested that a younger cellaress should be riding here and there in all kinds of weather, but she chose to carry on. And because she was as devout as ever, she allowed herself no respite from the convent's grueling daily round of offices.

Her life of prayer and work over, a nun dies in the convent's infirmary.

Last Illness

Her health worsened. She allowed herself to miss matins and lauds for a few days but would not enter the infirmary. Now, not surprisingly, she has fallen seriously ill and has difficulty breathing.

She feels she may be near death. A vision of being taken up to heaven has convinced her and also reassured her. She reflects that she is only in her forties but thinks of the young women, in their early twenties and teens, whom she has watched die in the nunnery.

She has asked that the nuns sing hymns. They also gather around her and recite the Lord's Prayer over and over.

She wishes to receive the last rites and Extreme Unction to set her on her eternal path and to be given the viaticum—the bread that is the body of Christ. Only priests can administer this. The sacristan rings a bell to summon a canon. He comes with three other clerics as witnesses and a lay brother.

Medieval Facts

In the *Necrology of Corpus Domini*, the story is told that for one dying nun in the convent, every one of the 110 nuns recited the Lord's Prayer 100 times each, for a total of 11,000 prayers. As if in response to knowing that they were doing that, the nun saw a host of faces shining around her—Saint Ursula and the 11,000 virgins.

Final Gathering

At the sound of a clapper, all the nuns come. The entire body of the convent is gathered around the dying nun's bed. The prioress asks a nun to describe a good quality of the dying sister as something to remember her by. The nun describes how the dying sister once remained motionless, not moving a limb, rapt in spirit for an entire day and night.

Another nun recalls the cellaress's love of poverty and recounts how she heard her say once that she would "rather have a devil in her cell than a shilling."

After listening to this recital of her virtues, the nuns wait for the cellaress to speak her last words, hoping to hear something significant or memorable. They are rewarded by hearing her say, "Obedience is the shortest path to eternal life."

Christ welcomes the faithful into heaven in this fourteenth-century Spanish painting.

Death Records

In the fifteenth-century *Necrology of Corpus Domini*, Sister Riccoboni records the deaths of members of the Venetian convent. The first entry, a brief one, seems particularly poignant:

❖ *In the first year that the convent was enclosed, Sister Paola Zorzi passed from this life at the age of thirteen. She was not yet professed. She was one of the women from San Girolamo.* ❖

San Girolamo was a convent of Augustinian nuns in Venice, from which a few women left for a new life at Corpus Domini.

41

GLOSSARY

Abbess/abbot ❖ the head of a nunnery or monastery

Bequest ❖ a legacy or a gift detailed in a will

Bishop ❖ from the Greek *episcopos*, meaning overseer; the highest rank of churchman in the diocese; a division of church terrain and control

Boondays ❖ extra days of work by demand on the lord's or lady's land

Canon ❖ clergy attached to a college church or cathedral; secular canons lived in their own houses; regular canons renounced private property

Cellaress ❖ a nunnery official responsible for food supplies and trade with the world outside

Chancel ❖ the main space at the east end of a church with the altar, separated by a screen from the nave

Chapterhouse ❖ a meeting space for the convent

Choir ❖ part of a church, in the chancel, where the nuns worship

Cloister ❖ covered open area around a courtyard or green space

Confession ❖ the private admission of sins to a priest

Convent ❖ a community of a religious order of nuns

Corrodians ❖ permanent paying guests who lived in separate small quarters at a convent

Diocese ❖ an area of churches, religious communities, and lay people under the control of a bishop

Divine offices ❖ religious services, usually seven or eight a day, sung and recited at specified hours

Due ❖ an amount to be paid

Dowry ❖ the money and goods a father gave his daughter when she married

Endowment ❖ a gift of money, usually to a religious or educational foundation

Eucharist ❖ the sacrament of the Lord's Supper

Feudalism ❖ the system of holding land in return for agreed services or works or money

Fine ❖ a fee or charge

General Chapter ❖ an annual meeting of the heads of religious houses

Hayward (or heyward) ❖ village official responsible for arranging the hay crop

Host ❖ the bread that is "the Body of Christ" in the holy communion

Investiture ❖ the act of formally putting someone into office

Laity ❖ from the Greek *laos*, people, the unordained (not in religious orders) people of the church

Manor ❖ a feudal estate tenanted by a lord, usually inherited, with its own manor court

Mark ❖ a coin worth 13 shillings, 4 pence

Mass ❖ the central religious service of the medieval church, enacting the ceremonial consumption of bread and wine, "the Body and Blood of Christ;" sung by the priest in Latin

Money ❖ Pounds (£), shillings, and pennies, or pence were the main coins used in Britain in medieval times. A mark was a coin worth 13 shillings, 4 pence.

Messuage ❖ House with its buildings and land

Monastery ❖ a place where nuns, monks, or both, live religiously away from society

Nave ❖ the main part of a church

Necrology ❖ a convent's "book of the dead" with brief accounts of each nun's last days

Novice ❖ no longer a postulant but not yet a nun

Obedientiaries ❖ people in a lesser position

Order ❖ religious communities belonged to one of a number of orders founded by different spiritual leaders, whose rules differed slightly

Payment in kind ❖ payment with articles of produce, such as eggs

Postulant ❖ a woman who expresses her desire to become a nun to an abbess

Pound (£) ❖ *See* Money

Priest ❖ the clerk in charge of the church; sometimes a rector or vicar

Prioress ❖ in Benedictine convents, the second in command after the abbess; the head of a religious house without the legal status of an abbey

Profession ❖ when a novice professes her desire to live according to the vows of an order, she becomes a nun

Psalter ❖ the Book of Psalms

Regular clergy ❖ those living according to the Rule of the order and usually in an enclosed community

Relic ❖ an object venerated by believers because of its associations with a saint or martyr

Rule ❖ a founder's or reformer's statement of basic values and practices for living in a particular order, usually enclosed but not always

Screen ❖ a division, usually of wood, between chancel and nave

Secular ❖ not separated from the world; secular clergy live in society

Shilling ❖ *See* Money

Tithe ❖ the annual payment due to the church or lord of one-tenth of a villein's produce

Toll ❖ the right to make strangers bringing goods to town pay an amount on what they brought in

Vestment ❖ religious garment, such as a cloak or robe

Villein ❖ a peasant who was tied to the land and farmed strips of a village's common field

Vows ❖ formal promises to God

Useful Medieval History Web Sites

www.mnsu.edu/emuseum/
history/middleages/
contents.html

Enter this Web site and choose a guide (knight, merchant, nun, or peasant) or topic and learn more about medieval life.

http://www.bcps.org/offices/
lis/models/medeurope/
sites.html

This Web site discusses the role of the church in medieval society, the crusades, religion in daily life, and monks and nuns.

http://www.mnsu.edu/
emuseum/history/
middleages/

Enter the Nun's Realm to learn about the medieval church, monks, and nuns.

Note to parents and teachers:
Every effort has been made by the publishers to ensure that the Web sites in this book are suitable for children, that they are of the highest educational value, and that they contain no inappropriate or offensive material. However, because of the nature of the Internet, it is impossible to guarantee that the contents of these sites will not be altered. We strongly advise that Internet access be supervised by a responsible adult.

TIME LINE

910	Abbey of Cluny founded.
ca. 1000	Scandia and Hungary converted to Christianity.
1066	William of Normandy invades England and is crowned king in December.
1066	England has 13 nunneries.
ca. 1080	The *Speculum Virginum (Mirror for Virgins)* is written for nuns.
1088	The papacy splits and there are two competing popes.
1096	The First Crusade begins.
1098	Cistercian order founded.
ca. 1100	A powerful religious revival in the twelfth and thirteenth centuries brings many women into religious communities.
1146	Saint Bernard of Clairvaux preaches (announces) the Second Crusade.
1162	In England, Thomas Becket is consecrated as Archbishop of Canterbury and quarrels with King Henry over the church's power.
1163	Cathedral of Notre Dame is begun in Paris.
1170	Thomas Becket is murdered by knights who believed this was what King Henry wanted.
1174	King Henry does penance for the murder of Thomas Becket.
1177	Amesbury nunnery is founded (perhaps as part of King Henry's penance) with a membership of French nuns.
1189	The Third Crusade begins and fails to capture Jerusalem.
1207	The Order of Saint Francis is formed.
1208	King John of England quarrels with the pope; the pope bans church services in England.
1208	Crusade against Albigensian heretics in France.
1215	King John signs the Magna Carta.
1216	Saint Dominic's order of Friar's—traveling preachers—is approved by the pope.
1217	The Fifth Crusade begins.
1230	King Henry III wages war in France.
1235	The black veil is stipulated for nuns.
1248	The Seventh Crusade begins.
1260	The cathedral is consecrated in Chartres, France.
1305	Clement V becomes the pope; the papacy moves to Avignon.
1348–1349	The bubonic plague (Black Death) spreads through Europe.
ca. 1350 on	Decline of nunnery membership after the plague.
1361	Europe experiences another outbreak of the plague.
1377	Avignon captivity of papacy ends.
1389	The first translation of the Bible into English.
1395–1436	Sister Riccoboni compiles *Chronicle and Necrology of Corpus Domini* in Venice.
ca. 1400	Christine de Pisan writes *Treasure of the City of Ladies* and other spiritual works.
ca. 1400	Beginnings of Modern Devotion movement in the Netherlands.
ca. 1400 on	Increasing ignorance of Latin and French among nuns; in England, the bishop's instructions are sent out in English.
1414–1418	The Great Papal Schism ends.
1450	Printing with moveable type is invented.
1490	The youngest daughter of King Edward IV enters a nunnery.
1530s	Dissolution of monasteries and nunneries in England.

INDEX

These are the lists of contents for each title in *Medieval Lives*: